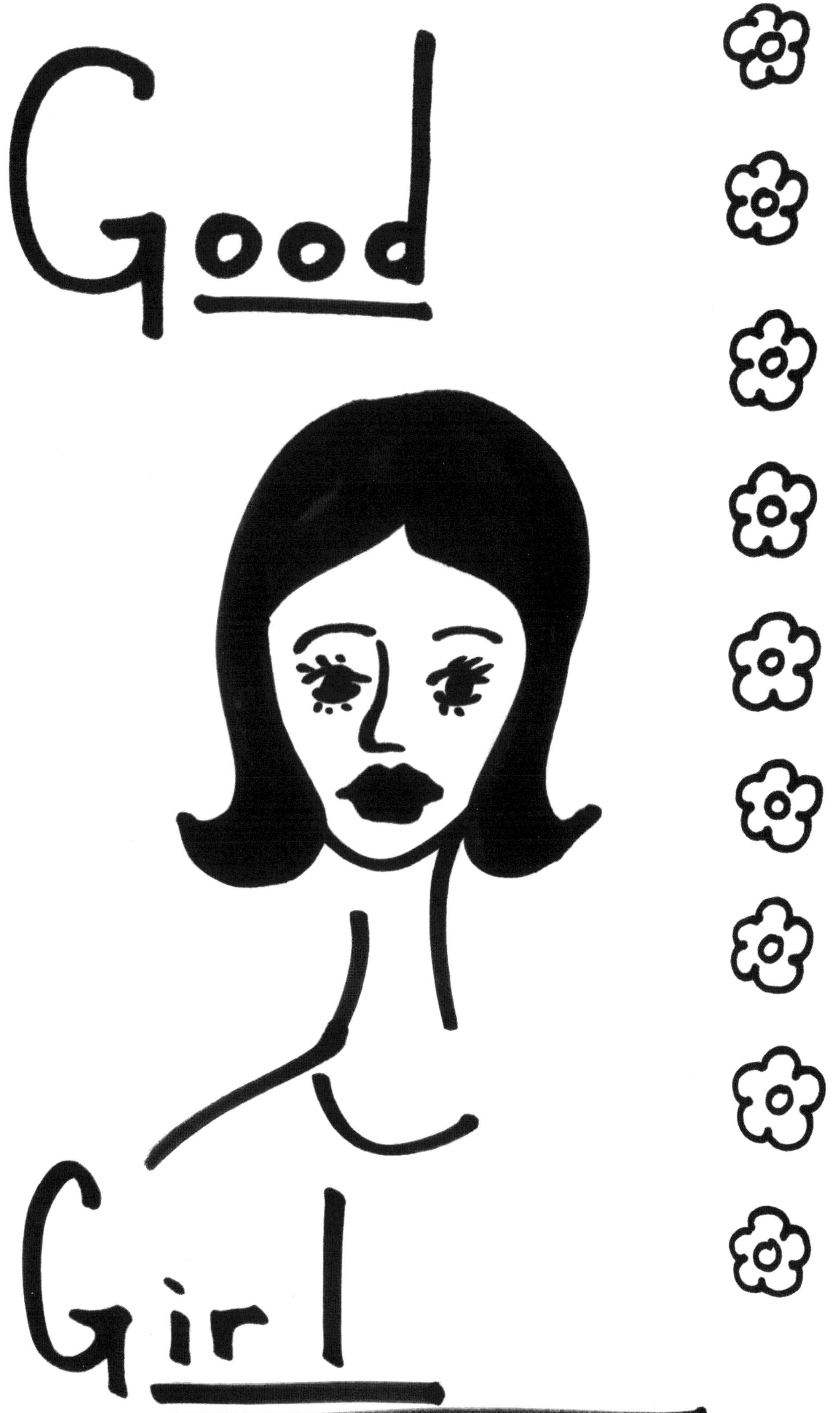
Good
Girl

The Good Girl Book

Pam Butler

Good Girl

STRUNG
OUT
with
South Forest

...uze YER CORRIGATION
+ ½

RING

GOOD

GIRL

MEGA

ADORABLE

(MONDAY)
SEPTEMBER-6-1993
9. A.M.

PLEASE SEND ME
INFORMATION ABOUT
YOUR GOOD GIRLS PROJECT
THANK YOU

8-30-93

What do i think of you
"good girl" project ??

Good Girl Project
P.O. BOX 1014
e Station
N.U. 10014

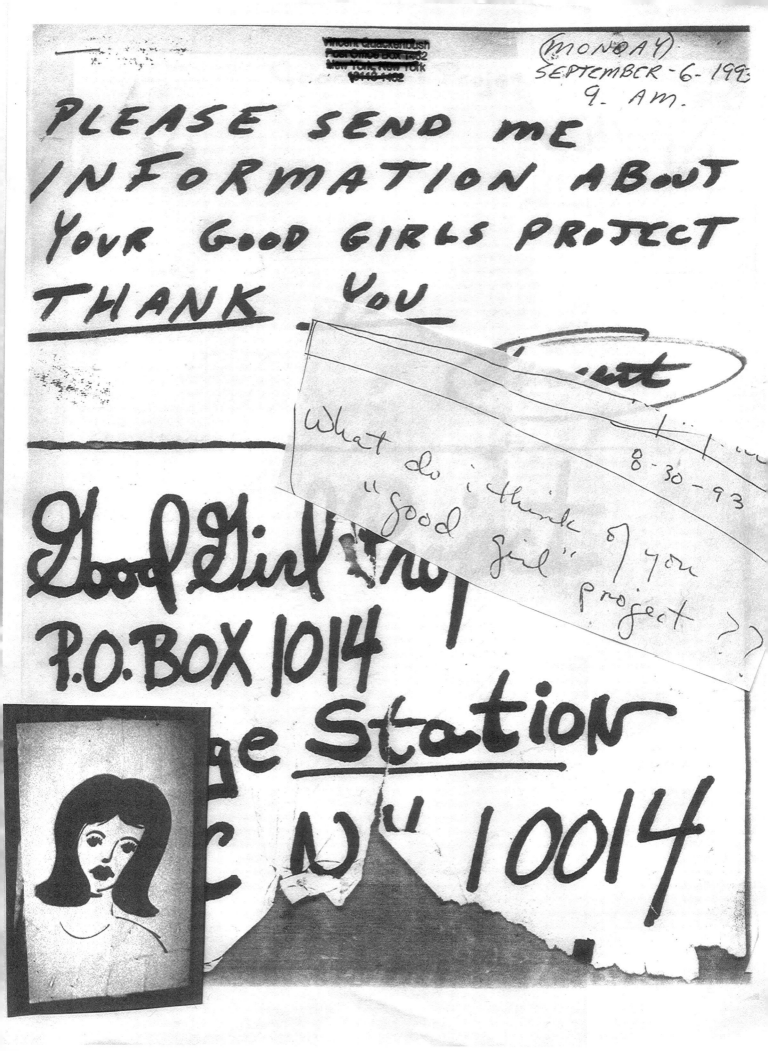

(P.S. I AM SINGLE)
34
9.12.59
6 FooT 2
165 PoUNDS

...nk you for your letter and for answering my
...d I did not copy your address correctly. or my
...the Mail.

I am Very interested in hearing
Good Girl Project. and seeing some of your
drawings. and Reading the stories Behind the PICTURES

there are so Many Questions I would like to ask. I am
Very Curious.

What is your Favorite Movie? I Will Plan to
Rent and Watch it.

How old are you? When is your Birthday?
Do you like Sports?

To Whom It May Concern:

I really hope I'm not bothering you or taking
up your time. I just wanted to write you about
the Good Girl Project. You see, I am a Good Girl

To Whom It May Concern at the "Good Girl Project":

For the past couple of years or so, you have been plastering
posters, both praiseworthy and blameful, but mostly offensive
throughout the city, concerning a young woman, and sometimes a
young man.

I would like to let you in on something which you really do not
deserve to know, given the inanity and utter stupidity of your
work, and that is, that in the highest spiritual sense, whether

COULD YOU TELL ME A LITTLE ABOUT THE

HISTORY & PHILOSOPHY BEHIND THE PROJECT (WHEN

DID IT START - WILL IT CONTINUE - HOW MANY

DIFFE   AIN

FOR T

SINCE

Dear Good Girl:

It is great to see you around town.
You are so very good. Especially
your hair!

I have tried hard to be a good
girl. But I haven't been very
successful. (maybe it's me

Good Girl Project:
   First reaction to the posters was "What's the point?"
... ...probably the point. Desire to put labels & closure on
... ..., which the
recall that too

Good Girl Project
PO BOX 1014
Village Station
NYC   NY 10014

Aug 28th, 1993

Dear Jamie,

Thank-You for your wonderful
letter & your many comments
... ...

Dear Katherine,
      Please excuse that its taken me so
long to answer your wonderful letter. You see,
I too, can only try to be a truly good girl.
Sometimes its easier to just be a pumpkin.

Dear Emily,

I was truly delighted with your
wonderful letter. It was very inspirational.
Thanks awfully for taking the time to
write it and please accept my
appologies for not immeditaly respo...
It was so very nice to hear from
someone who so very clearly

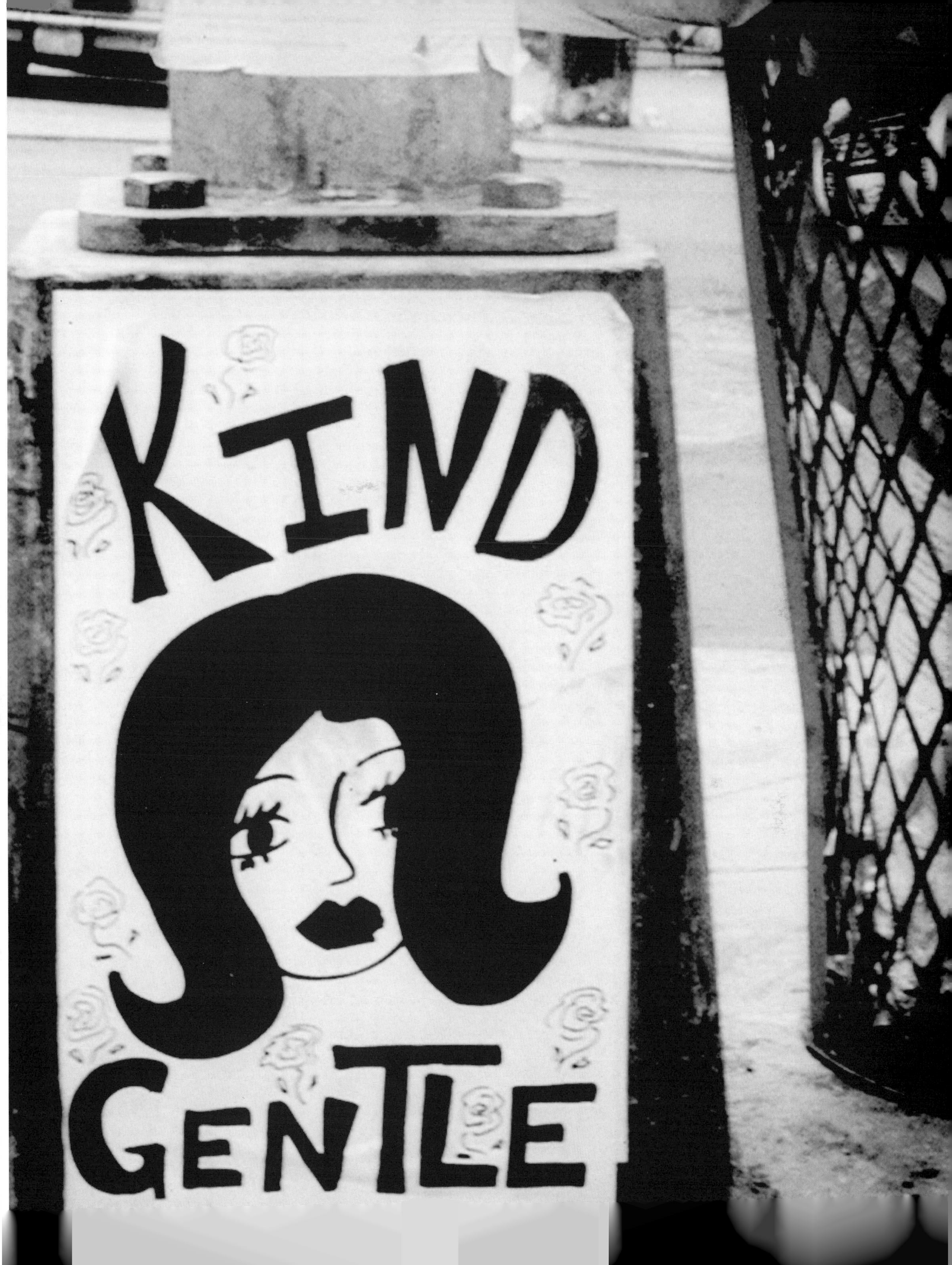
KIND
GENTLE

Gracious

Delicate

Suppose I Was Dead

A GOOD GIRL POEM

VERY GOOD.
VERY GOOD.
Always a very good
girl.
Nice, kind

Wishing
Willing, Willful,
Wanton, Wanting, Waiting.
WAIT
Whiner, Whimper
Willing, Witch, Whore

Whore, Willing

HELPFUL
Helper, Helpless, Hopeless
Hopeful
Very good.

Always a very good girl.
Nice, kind

CUNT

A Cunt
A smelly cunt
Cutie
Very cute

DOG
A Dog
Bark, Bark Bark
And
Deceitful Dolly Darling

Sweet

Sugar, Candy, Delicate,
Delicious

Thinnest
Prim, Proper, Prissy

Prick, Dick
Dickhead

Dreamboat
Superman
(I WANT)

Hero — or
Sissy - Wimp
(whiner, whimper)
Deviant
Pig — Perverted - Pussy

PUSSY

Soft
Simple, Slow, Slut

SUPPOSE

Suppose it was always all right
You were always very beautiful
Suppose every body always liked
you.

I am nice
Really (and reasonable)

AND

SUPPOSE I AM A PRINCESS
Her Royal Highness
Suppose a knight in shinning Armour.
I WANT A KNIGHT IN SHINNING ARMOUR.

Shinning

Shinning brightly for me
Shinning brightly just for me

DREAMER

Brazen

Nag
(Bag Ha

Naughty

NICE
Like I said I am a very nice girl
Good, Kind
Courteous, Gracious
Fickle - Frivolous - Flighty
AND

Suppose I could fly?
Like a bird
RIGHT NOW
Anywhere I might want to go.

I have 3 wishes
WISH
(wishing, willful)

Deceived

AGAIN

Savage.
Bold

He is a savage.
My savage.
My Savior
My Mega Man
My Stallion, My Stud

A Bastard
A Brute
A Creep

A CREEP

Forever and ever
AND EVER

Always

Taken
Kept

I want a Sugar Daddy
A Candyman
MY OWN BOY TOY

I WANT TO BE

A kept woman.
She gets whatever she wants.

A BIMBO

Fluffy
FAST
Loose - Cheap
Soiled
Shameless, Shameless
Pushy

And a pussy
Pussy, pussy

SCREAMER - SHRILL

SUPPOSE I DIE RIGHT NOW?
SUPPOSE I WAS NEVER BORN?

I told you
I have been
A very nice girl.
Obedient - Kind - Good
Respectful and Sweet.

There should be a happy ending

SERVICEABLE

Flowers

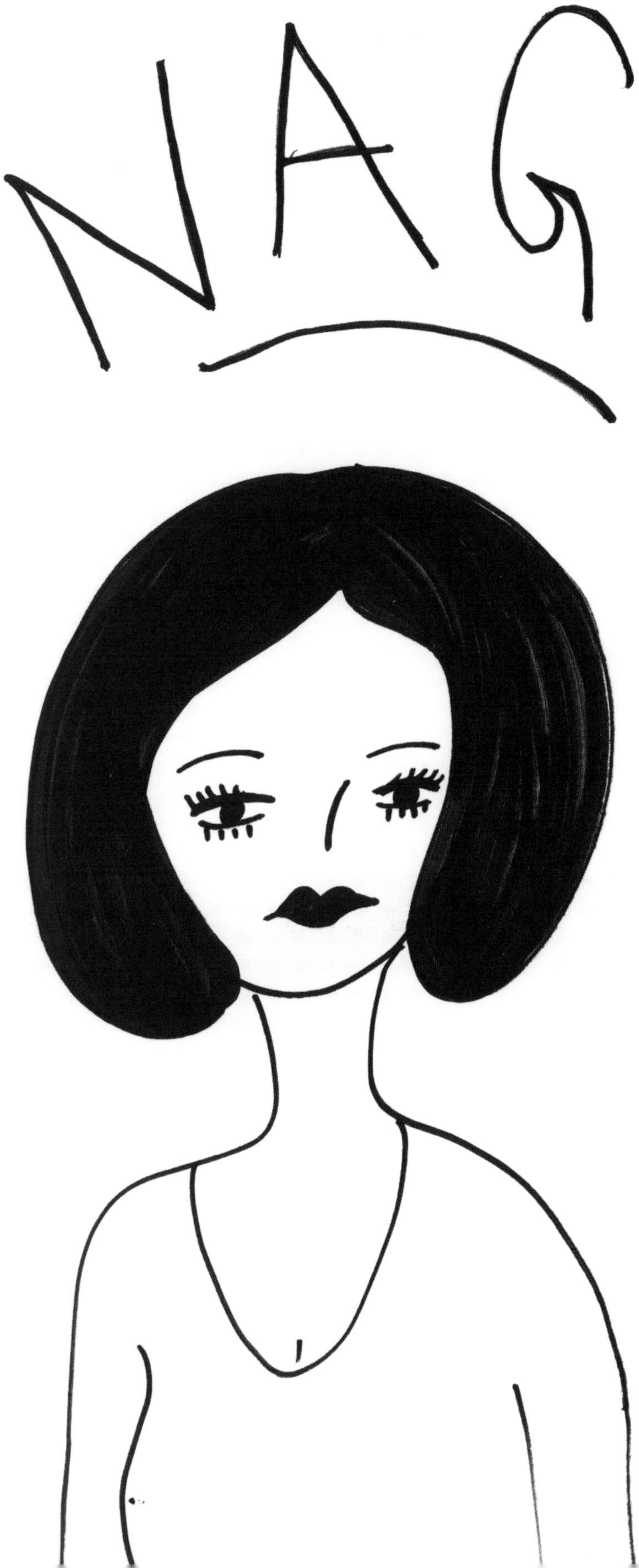
NAG

BAG

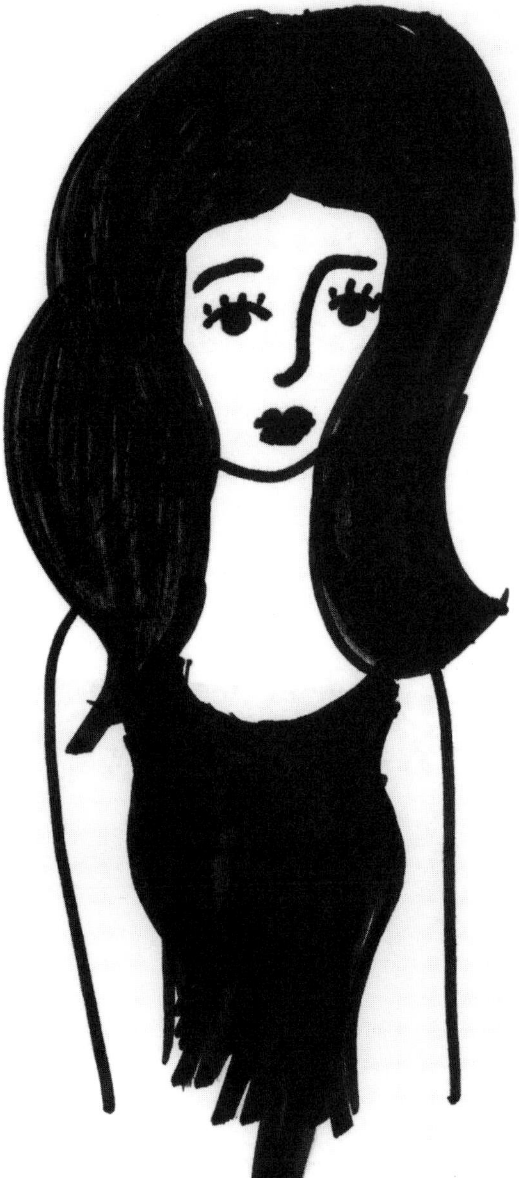

HAG

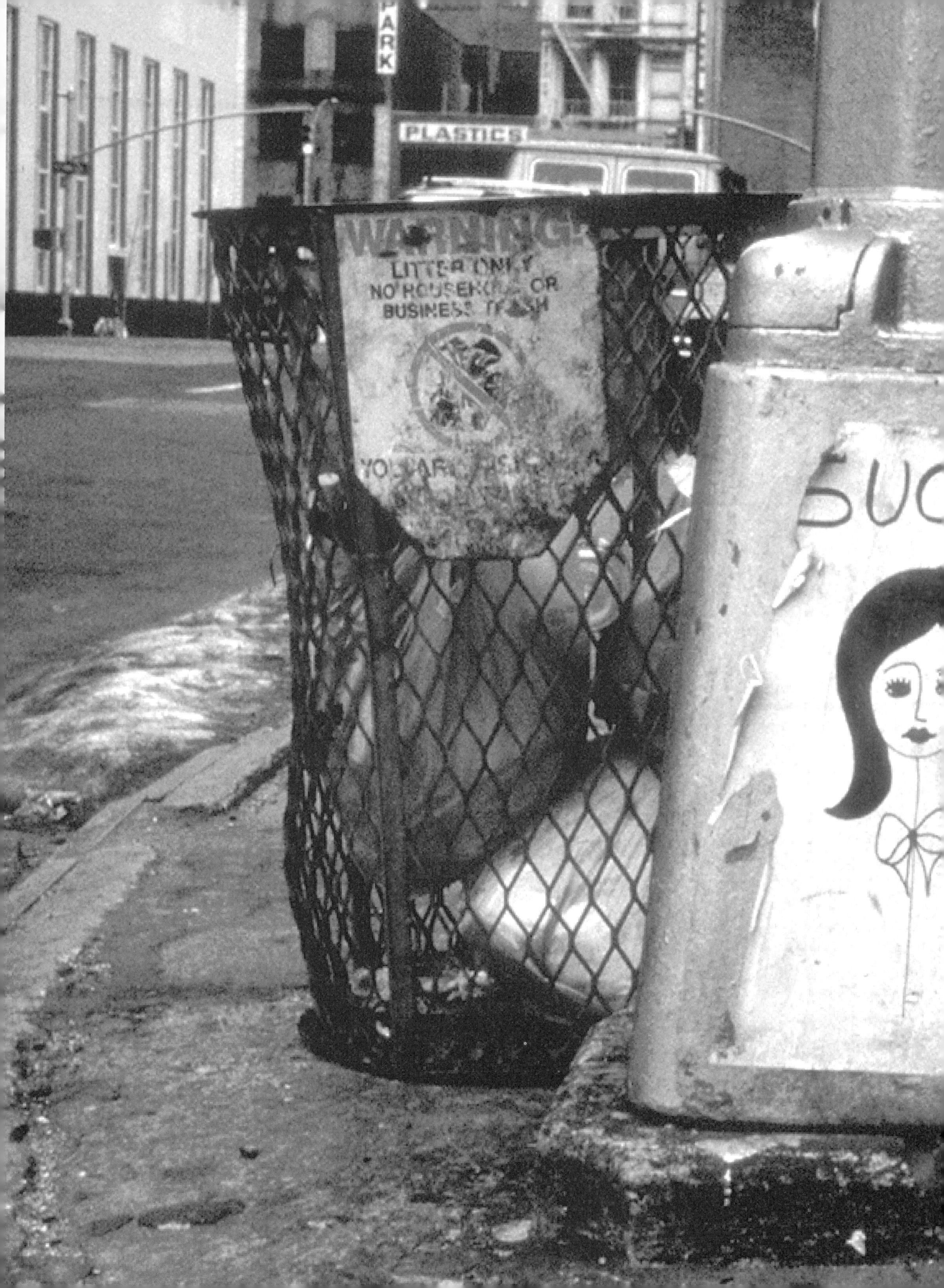
PARK
PLASTICS
WARNING
LITTER ONLY

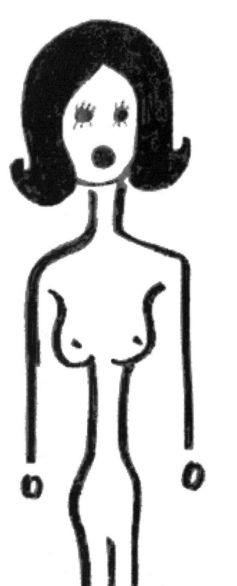

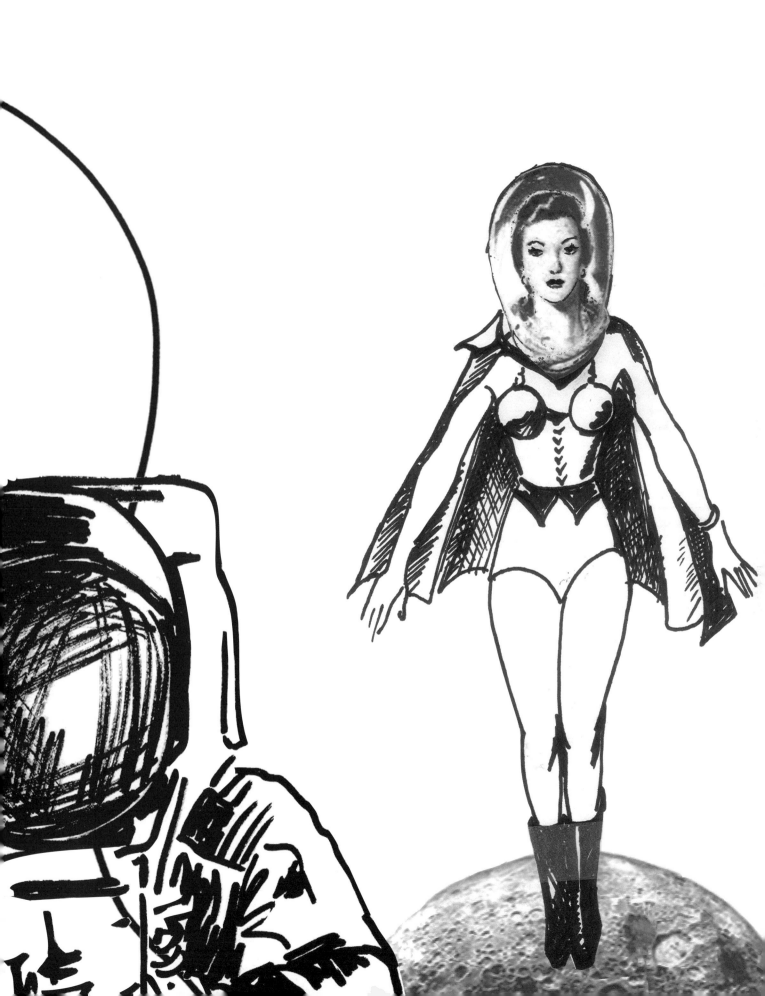

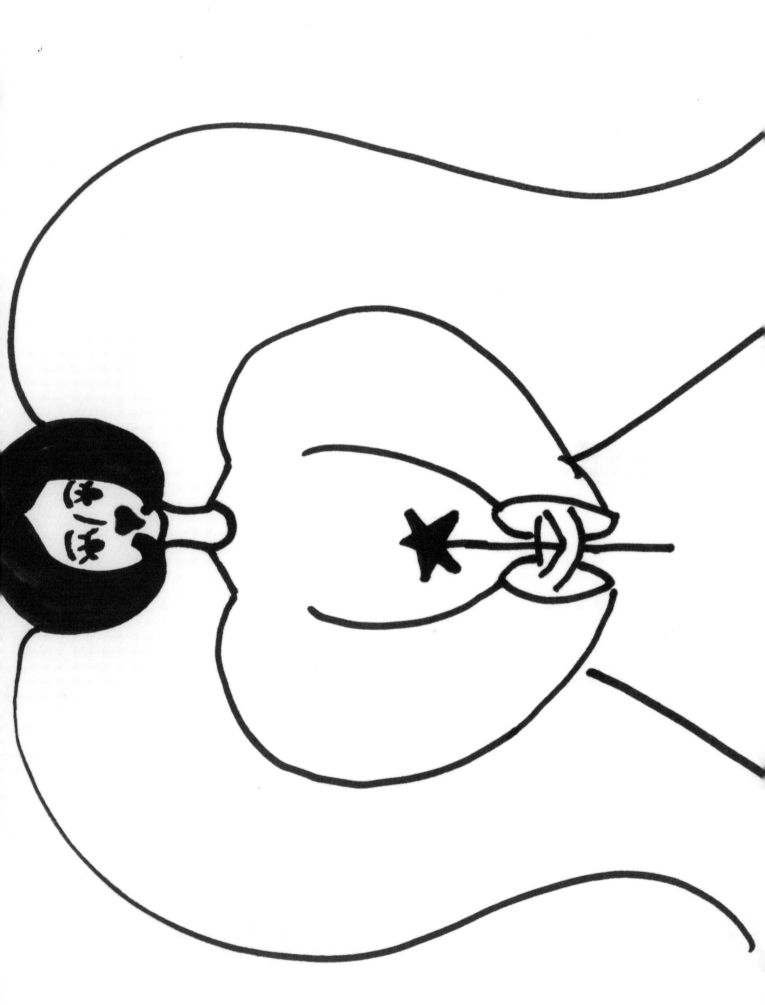

Wishtu

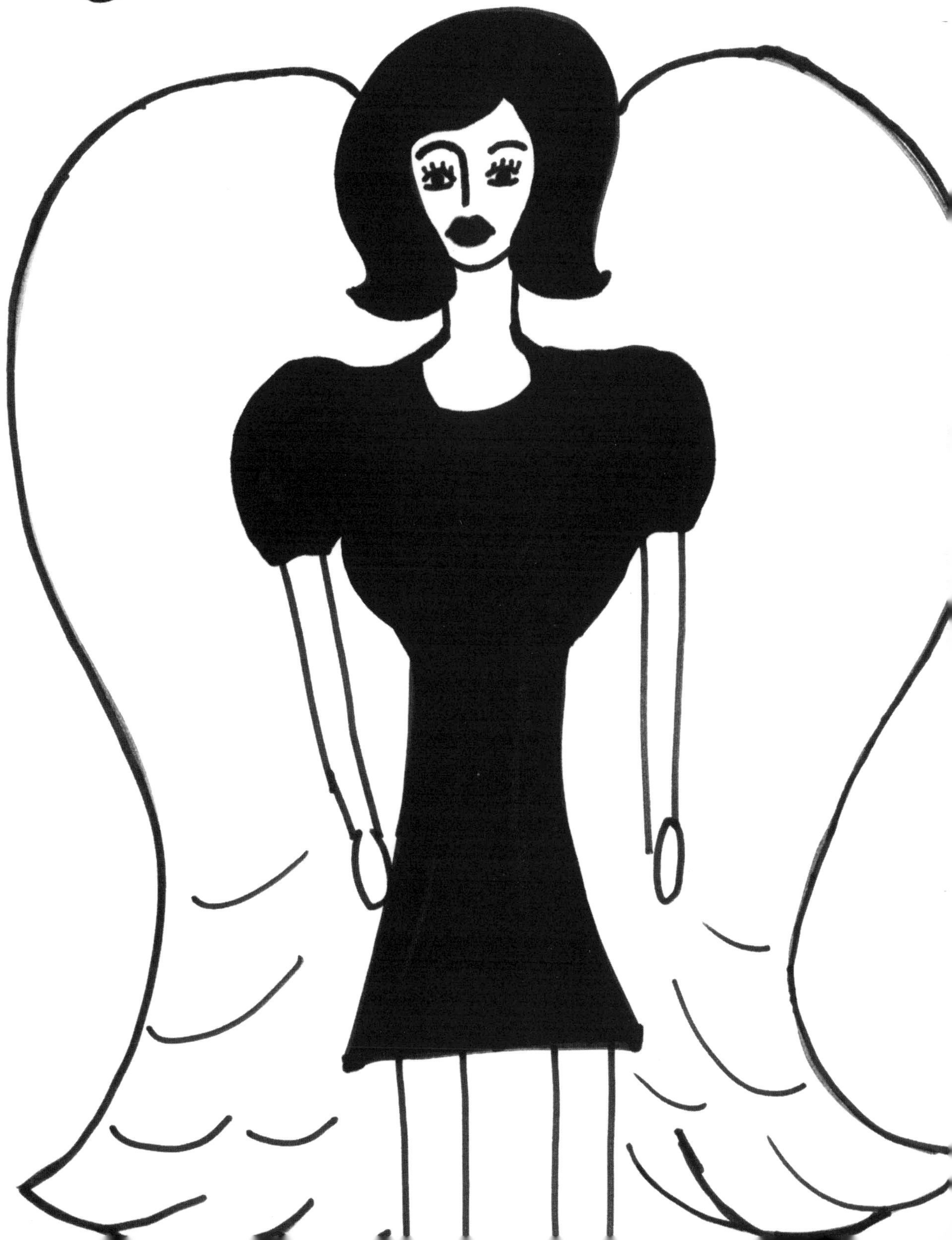

Moon

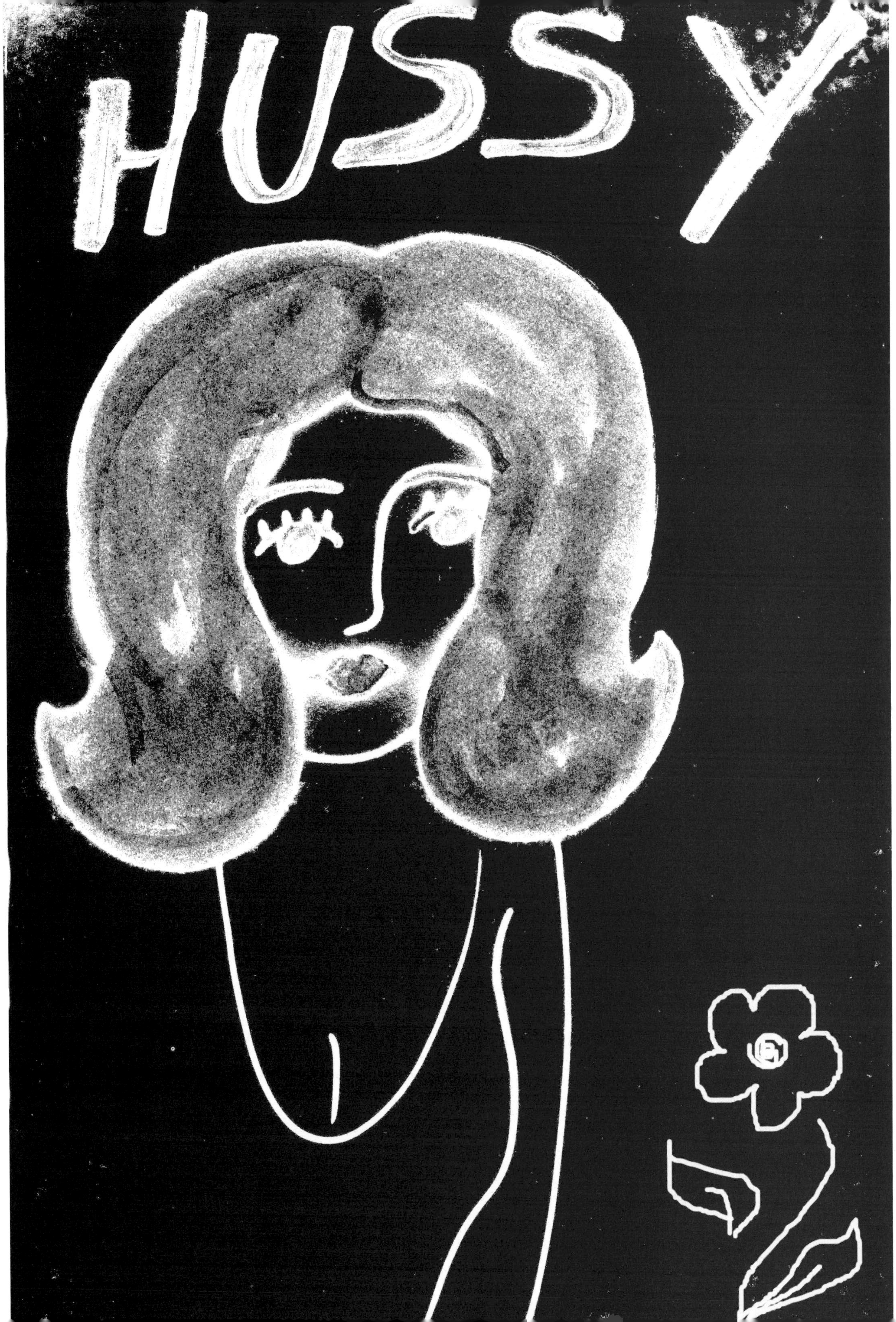
HUSSY

LIVE

204 VARICK STREET (CO

MY ROMANTIC POEM

He had a mysterious air
A distant allure
Yet his presence filled the room
His laugh captivated
Smoldering gray eyes
Burned deep
Deep into the hidden recesses of her soul
She was stripped
Naked by his gaze
Emotionally
Dazed, exposed, defenseless, helpless, vulnerable
Swept into strange currents from unknown longings
Floating on waves of ecstasy

The summer breeze ruffled his sun streaked hair
In the fading glow of the twilight
She had been waiting for this moment
It was
The magic transformation of her
Drab and dreary life
She stood on polished marble floors
Lush silken Persian carpets
She was enveloped in
The scent of roses
The pounding surf
The canopied bed
The satin sheets
The heat of his desire
The warmth of his lips
She no longer resisted,
She could no longer resist
She walked into his arms she felt her
Transformation – transformed
Every wish granted
Dreams come true.

She shook
Shaky, softly
was kissed
A ravenous kiss
Stealing breath
Driving her mad with passion
Harsh dark passion

Bold passion
Demanding, sensuous, insistent
Astonishing
Imposing - Overwhelming

The last fragile thread of all resistance
Unraveling.
She was possessed by
forgotten desires
and by
His tormenting needs
She abandoned herself into
His devouring
Urgency.

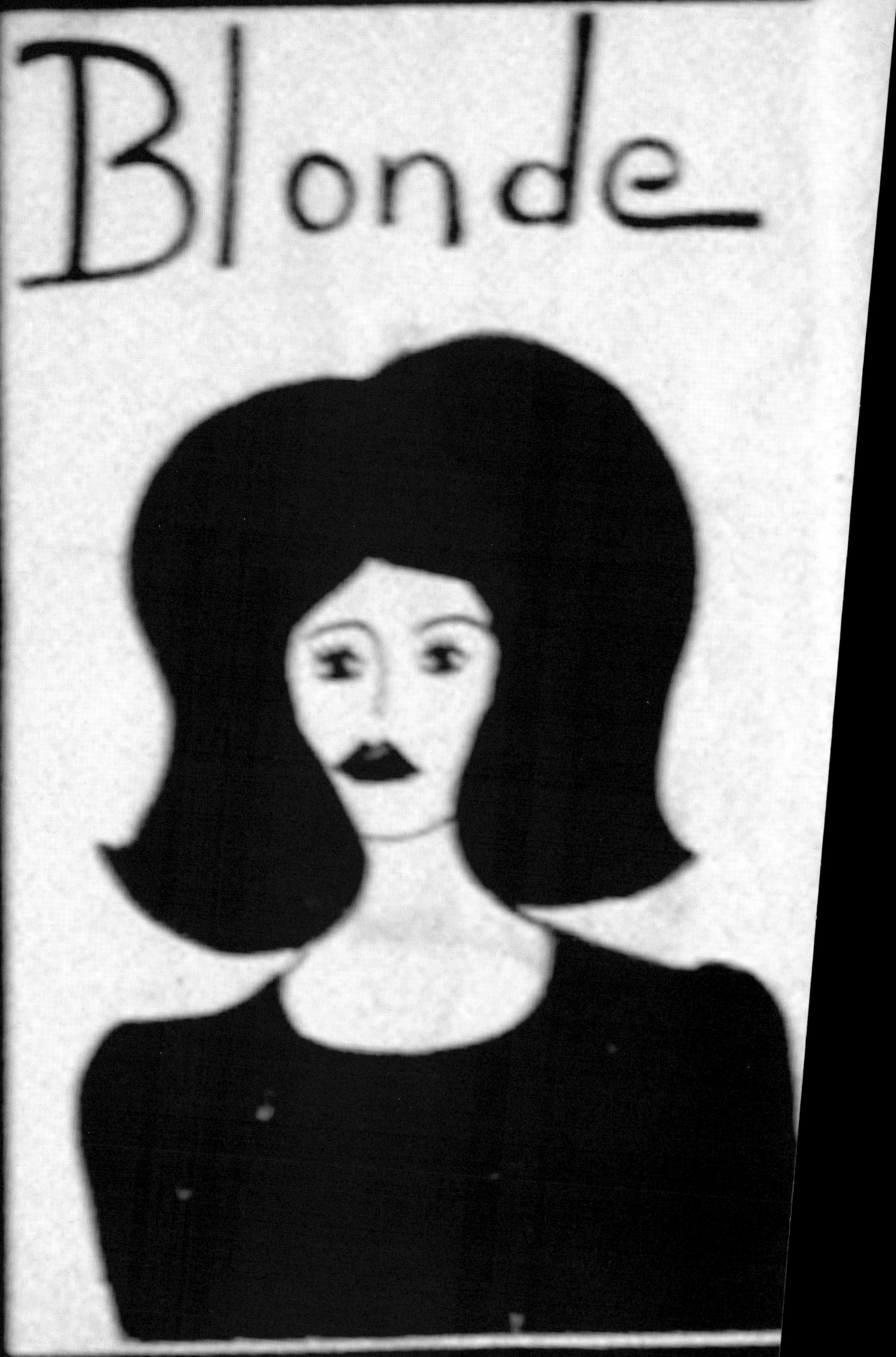
Blonde

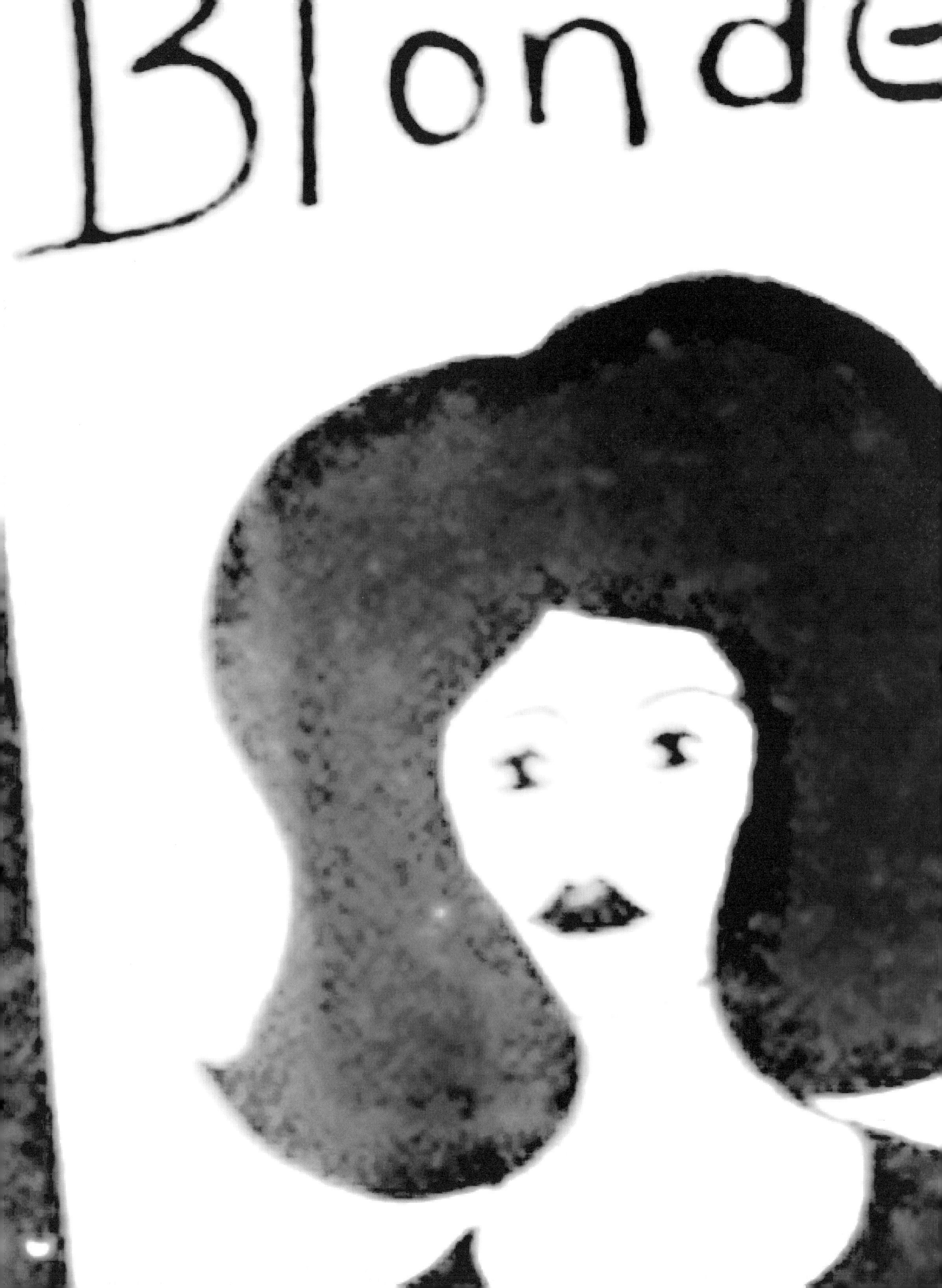
Blonde

Suppose a Knight in Shining Armor

Prince Charming

Good Boy
Prince Charming
Suppose I was a Princess
Suppose a Knight in Shining Armor

I FOCUS ON THE POSITIVE

I AM JOY FILLED

I CHOOSE TO BE KIND

I AM VERY BEAUTIFUL

I ATTRACT PROSPERITY

M SURRONDED BY MY ABUNDANCE
M VERY BEAUTIFUL
REATE MY DREAMS NOW
W I CREATE MY WILDEST DREAMS
MBODY GREAT SUCCESS AND TRIUMPH
M A WINNER
M VERY BEAUTIFUL
M SURRONDED BY POSITIVE ENERGY AND LIGHT
M A WINNER
M VERY BEAUTIFUL
TRACT LOVE AFFECTION AND GREAT WEALTH
M A WINNER
M AN ACCEPTING PERSON
M A FORGIVING PERSON
OLLOW MY BLISS
VISION MY HIGHER GOOD
HOOSE LOVE AND JOY
M AT PEACE WITH MYSELF
M INFINITLY CONTENT AND SATISFIED - NOW -
HT NOW I AM INFINITLY CONTENT AND TOTALLY SATISFIED
M VERY BEAUTIFUL
M VERY VERY BEAUTIFUL
M A WINNER
M ALWAYS A WINNER
M SURRONDED BY POSITIVE ENERGY AND LIGHT
M GUIDED AND PROTECTED BY ANGELS
M SURRONDED BY MY GUARDIAN ANGELS
M VERYVERY BEAUTIFUL
LL JOYFULLY AND EASILY REACH MY GOALS
M VERY VERY BEAUTIFUL
TRACT PROSPERITY
TRACT SUCCESS AND PROSPERITY WITH ALL I DO
M VERY VERY BEAUTIFUL
M GUIDED BY THE DIVINE
PECT GOOD FORTUNE
M ALWAYS A WINNER
DIATE WARMTH AND LOVE
M A DYNAMIC EXCITING PERSON
M SURRONDED BY MY GUARDIAN ANGELS
M VERY VERY BEAUTIFUL
M ALWAYS VERY VERY BEAUTIFUL
GUARDIAN ANGELS ARE VERY BEAUTIFUL
M A FORGIVING POITIVE PERSON
E THANKS FOR A QUICK & SUBSTANIAL INCREASE IN MY FINACIAL INCOME NOW
HT NOW
HT NOW
M A PERFECT BEAUTIFUL WINNING PERSON

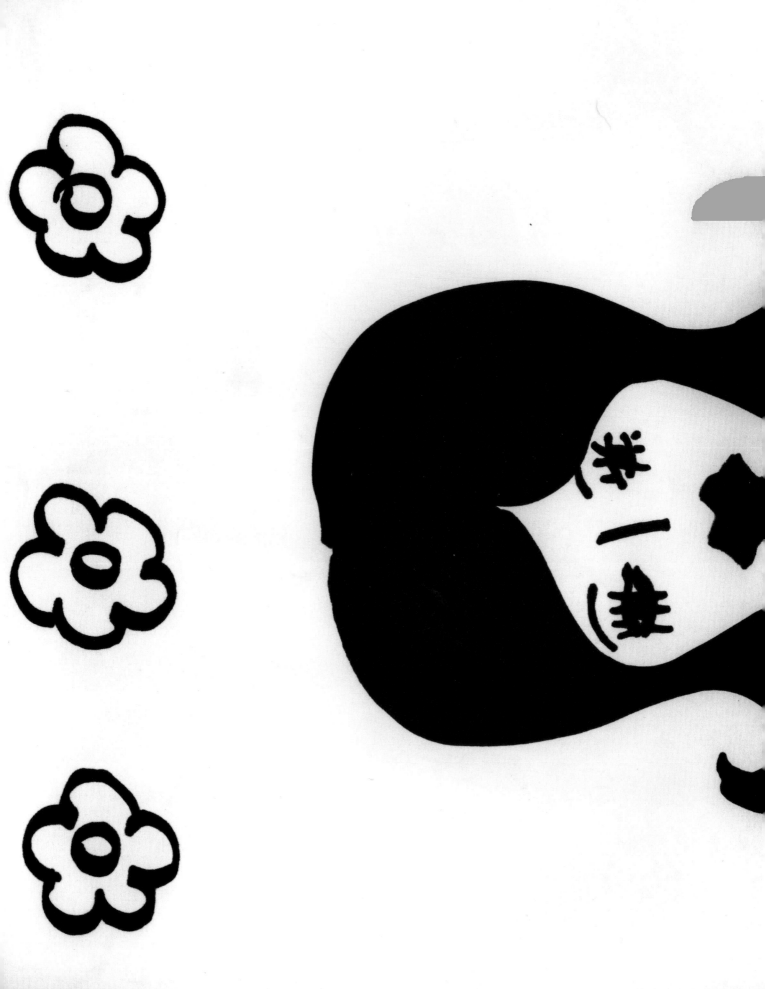

Other Things To Remember:

1) Someone has to take the blame and if not you who will? After all you know deep down that it's really your fault anyhow.

2) Accept what ever you happen to get; after all you don't ever want to appear too fussy or needy.

3) If you aren't always sorry people might think you're never really sorry at all.

4) Always appear helpless; otherwise you might have to ask for help. It's never good to have to ask. You want people to do things for you only when they really really want to and need to.

5) Never put yourself first, others needs are always more important than yours.

6) Don't ever call attention to yourself or you might be seen as behaving badly (outrageous, shameful, scandalous, disgraceful).

ART
Sweetness
NAG
BAG
HAG
Bitch
witch
PUSSY
Good Girl

TART

sweetness

Be Perfect Pussy

Good Girl

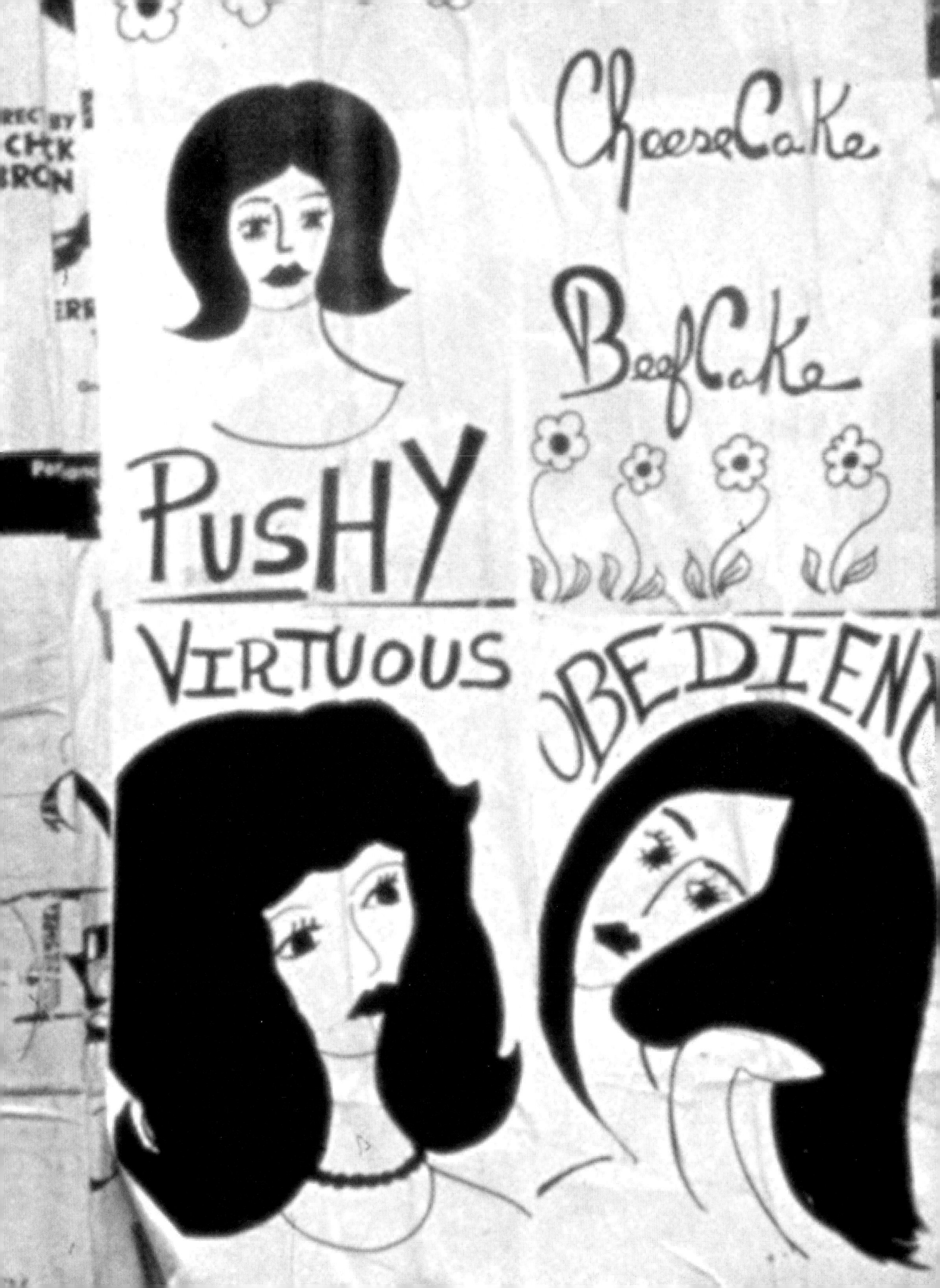

CheeseCake
BeefCake
PUSHY
VIRTUOUS
OBEDIEN

Yours truly,

them of all at laugh and responses, for begging probably are You
letter. this by offended be not will you mention, any of worthy
really you if course, Of this. like something on money and
time their wasting stop will "Project Girl Good" the of charge in
whoever that and subside, day one will anger your that hope I

her. affecting praising
or name-calling any let not will she as insofar stronger her

name-calling, which you have ... very good ... has this made

Dear Good Girl:

It is great to see you around town. You are so very good. Especially your hair!

I have tried hard to be a good girl. But I haven't been very successful. (maybe it's my cowlick?) So, I've tried to be in every... and, frankly, I'm not long-established ... at ... girl ... either.

1. Always say "That's OK," "I don't mind," or "No, it was my fault," whether someone has stepped on your toe or cancelled a dinner date at the last minute.

2. Feel bad a lot, but never take your bad moods out on other people (then they might not like you).

3. Feel responsible for everyone else's feelings.

4. Feel confused about your own feelings.

5. Smile a lot.

Hi:

I'm writing because I just love seeing your drawings eve...
I go. There should be more street art that's what I say.
My friends and I were wondering if the artist is a woman/a gr...
of women(if the answer is yes I shall be treated to a night
on the town...).

An Admirer,

If
you don't love
me
no one will

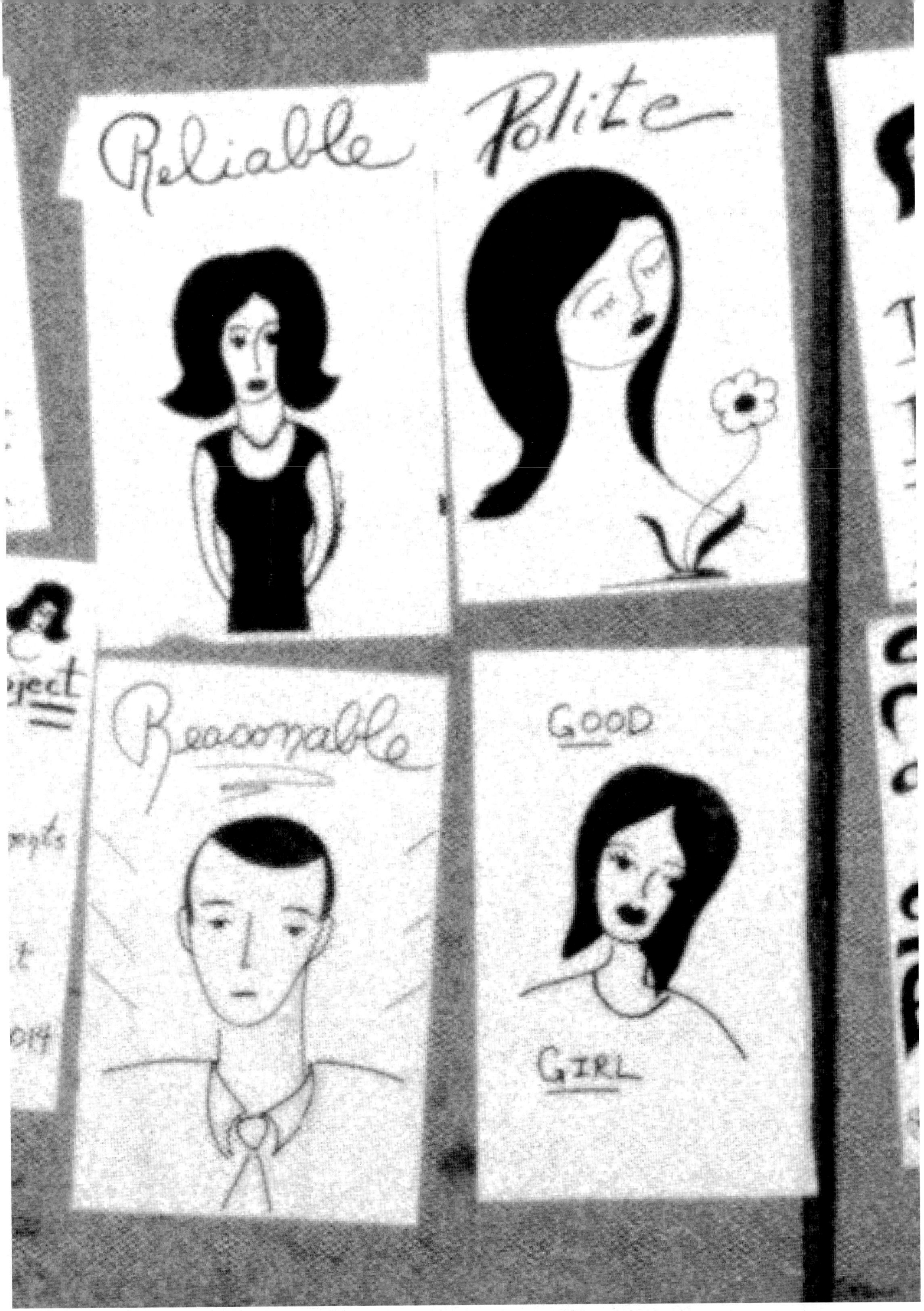
Reliable
Polite
Reasonable
GOOD
GIRL

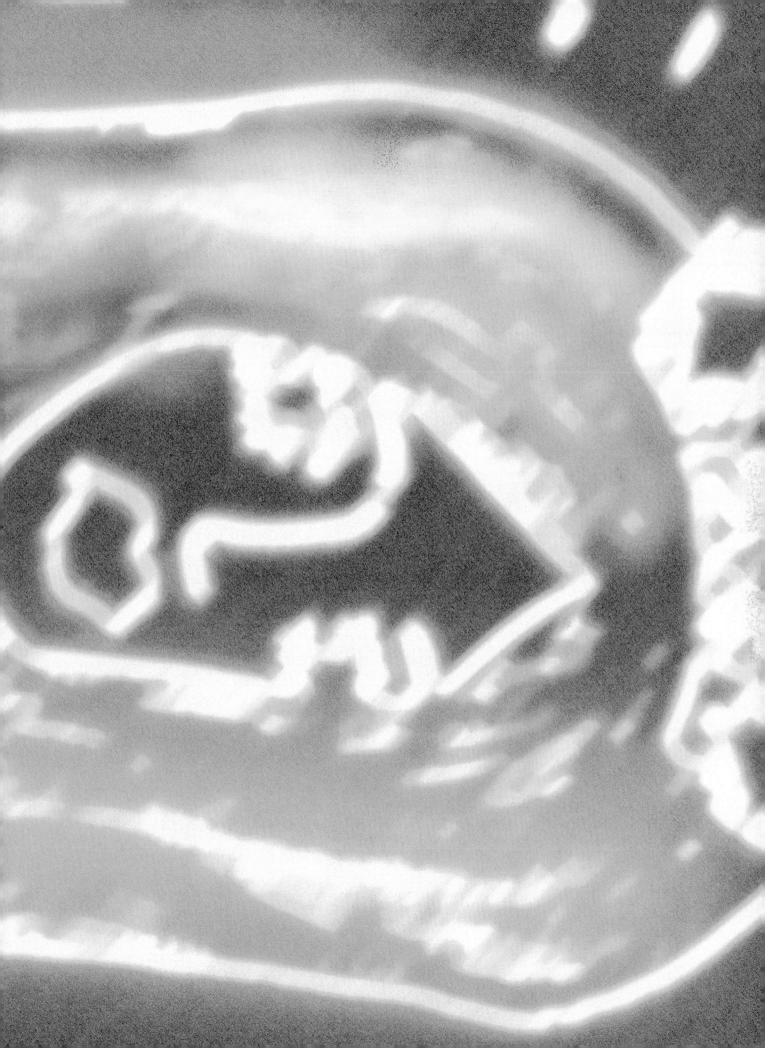

When I think
of you all my
failures become
perfectly clear
and I imagine
jumping off a long
and high suspension
bridge

Suppose you were happy forever after

Suppose the KX Maworld

Kitten

Suppose
I
Was a
Princess

Reasonable

NICE

DAINTY

Pretty Boy

DEAR GOOD GIRLS,

PLEASE SEND ME INFO ABOUT
YOUR ORGANIZATION ASAP. I'M VERY
INTERESTED! SEND ME A POSTER TOO.
I'M READY TO HELP!

PRETTY GIRL

ISBN #978-0-615-37613-4
copyright Pam Butler 2010
www.pambutlerart.com

Published by
mooresartpress209
250 Moore Street
Brooklyn, NY 11206
info@mooresartpress209.com

printed in an edition of 1,000
(25 of which are signed and numbered with hand drawn
slip cover and 2 original drawings added to book)
at Linco Printing Inc, Long Island City, NY